AGAINST HEAVEN

Winner of the 2021 Academy of American Poets First Book Award
Selected by Claudia Rankine

Sponsored by the Academy of American Poets, the First Book Award
is given annually to the winner of an open competition among
American poets who have not yet published a book of poems.

AGAINST HEAVEN

poems

KEMI ALABI

Graywolf Press

This publication is made possible, in part, by the voters of Minnesota through a Minnesota State Arts Board Operating Support grant, thanks to a legislative appropriation from the arts and cultural heritage fund. Significant support has also been provided by the McKnight Foundation, the Lannan Foundation, the Amazon Literary Partnership, and other generous contributions from foundations, corporations, and individuals. To these organizations and individuals we offer our heartfelt thanks.

MINNESOTA
STATE ARTS BOARD

CLEAN
WATER
LAND &
LEGACY
AMENDMENT

Published by Graywolf Press
250 Third Avenue North, Suite 600
Minneapolis, Minnesota 55401

www.graywolfpress.org

Published in the United States of America

ISBN 978-1-64445-082-6

2 4 6 8 9 7 5 3 1
First Graywolf Printing, 2022

Library of Congress Control Number: 2021940580

Cover design: Kapo Ng

Cover art: Llanor Alleyne, *Seraphina*, collage on paper

CONTENTS

When we say abolish police. We also mean the cop in your head and in your heart.   —Tourmaline

The erotic is a measure between the beginnings of our sense of self and the chaos of our strongest feelings. It is an internal sense of satisfaction to which, once we have experienced it, we know we can aspire. For having experienced the fullness of this depth of feeling and recognizing its power, in honor and self-respect we can require no less of ourselves.   —Audre Lorde

AGAINST HEAVEN

How to Fornicate

I.   After killing your god, hotbox the gun smoke.
Cough out any vestigial prayer.

Remember that spooky shit Ole Boy hissed
mid-smite, bullet-plowed, curling away. It's true.

You belong to the fire now.

II.   Lose your Bible—

book of napkins to fold
so the hungry busy their hands.

Stop circling garden gates for scraps
when a harvest splits your hips.

III.   Your booty a whole altar call—

sickle-pitched hallelujah
Blessed Queers are born screaming.

Become the most honest song they will ever sing
(or the worst or both or never mind).

IV.   When street preacher rebukes your thighs TV
after-school-specials your mouth Adam

tweets fuck that nappy-headed ribsplint Snake
primes the bite you die inside, say

my own my own my own my own.

V.   Choir everything. Tenor the roses.
       Alto the mulch. Mezzo the flies.

       Bass your bed, mountain they go tell on.

VI.   Disenchant the talismans of gods you love and leave.

       Spit flesh back to wafer.
       Left-swipe eyes you caught and kept.

       Feed them to the cross pyre,
       blood rewarming.

VII.   Remember Genesis—

       the worlds and little deaths you build
       with just your breath and hands,

       silhouettes that singe the walls
       with new maps to salvation

       till even the floorboards buck
       and cry *Jesus.*

       Even the windows blush
       and say *amen.*

Against Heaven

double golden shovel with Saba and Nick Hakim

There's Earth. Amethyst. Cherries in heat. Trees drooling sugar. Midnight's blue song. So what heaven? That kingdom wholed by a coy god's touch? Where green and the river began? If all-father tells it, first you slave and shiver and shuck and die and die for heaven's around-back gate to budge loose at the bent speck of you—lies. No doors, no lines. Look right: me and mine kissed alive—greening. Curl up and chime against us—the river's born here.

WE WOULD HEX THE PRESIDENT BUT

our bloom game too strong / altar stays red candle cinnamon-lit
sweet flicker cracking into prance / stays portal door warmed ajar
spell-flung darkward / *would* but we so black we lightless

no mirrors / so touchsoundfood our cedar smoke drumkicks
the body back to gospel / drumsticks the body smacked in mouthfuls
the room perfumes with our funkbrightwild / *would* but our skin yams

plush mothers cackling juice dripping / and this just our first slow branch
ascending / *would* but neighbors to dine and unstranger / rootbind into kin
a nation of misalphaed wolf carcass to climb through / *would* hex their new head

that neverman / rot reeking the soil / but who'd feed these seeds
that wet orange howl just compost slime returning returning
the sky glows red candle / air soots and sludges darkward / still

our funkbrightwild / block by block our tangling tangling
we *would* hex the damned born-dead but billions still alive / cored and alive
threshed concave and still sweet flickers / *would* but *who needs these feasts?*

Love Poem -1: Chicago (CST) to Bangalore (GMT+5:30)

Then love was a phone ding's dopamine thimble
instead of revolution, our green and singing world.

My day your night. Your day
my husking, skin to bark to sap rot.

No pixels, no disembodied voice teched toward me
reassembled you *here*.

Both feet missing. Inner ears gone.
Top of your head, merely suspect.

Each eye's prism, flattened.
The geometry of your chest, lost math.

The godweld between us taffied,
split back to word and light.

Its reconfigured data—
your slick hologram—

my dearest friend who refused
to touch me.

black as:

wound

Not all of us survived. Grief came home, back to our throats, our lungs. Grief been black—blue black. Tires-bald-between-work-and-home black. Monday-through-Sunday-double-shifts black. Asked about those visions—if spirits still slicked my mother's sleep—and she said she's too tired to dream. Too-tired-to-see-nothing-but black. Grief came home, to our lead-thick water, our Big-Mac-breakfast-greasing-the-way-between-work-and-home-and-work-and-home black. Begged her to take sick time, but not-a-day-off-in-ten-years black. Said the place would fall apart without her, but not-a-raise-in-ten-years black. Needs the health insurance, dad used nine diapers all before noon, don't-make-pill-boxes-big-enough black, and the co-pays alone. Not all of us survive. Not all living is surviving. A virus can't take what they already stole: our land, our labor, our language, our magic, our minds, our time, our time. But all my mother's mail tries to tell her what she owes. How much will her burial cost, death-another-debt black. Grief-a-bill-where-the-body-was black. News all markets and borders and shouts and nothing we can live on, no-news-still-bad-news black. Learned about the virus on the clock when the packages he shipped became essential. Learned about the virus when pastor got sick, though he was covered in The Blood, though she made third, fourth jobs of prayer. Learned about the virus when the cough came, when the clinic wouldn't answer the phone, remembered what the ER cost last time, so I just stayed home. When even the stores in the white neighborhoods had nothing on the shelves. When the calls from the cousins up in county came, and even their pitch was a fever.

portal

and even their pitch was a fever

became essential   shouts
        we can live on

        a bill the body
        owes for our magic

        all living
        would fall apart without

        our Black
greasing the way between

                home and   *home*

grief   our thickwater spirit

        vision double

        shifts Black
        motherblue

        back home

Voice Clear As

When my mom discovers heaven's just a noise festival

the godchoir of all her loves breathing
unsnagged by asthma or Newport-dragged lung

the true song life makes untethered from a body
tugged at last from the men who hold its reins

will she blame her pastors (like I did)
for Sunday portraits of pooled white gold?

Will she miss the wooden flute of her body,
mourn the days corner-propped, cloaked in dust

too pious to disturb a room's skin cells
and stray hair with her sound

snapped awake at the nightmare of a slip fringe,
the private note sung aloud?

Or, unburdened by hell,

will she exhale
and hear the bells?

The Lion Tamer's Daughter Learns the Rules

Your body is the inside of the nearest man's fist.
Walk to the store & back without disappearing.

Pick one:
hoop
leash
whip

When someone bumps into you, roll the die.

Even:
apologize

Odd:
apologize

Pick one:
circus
zoo
parade

Pick two:
missing
gutted
stuffed

Your voice is a sidewalk crack, keeper of the mother spine.
Speak & it breaks.
Scream & *poof*—
salt.

Pick one:
pass
pass

Pick two:
pass
pass

Winner takes
shape.

Loser:
salt!

To start:

Sunday Closet

Sure, the exalted drag of dresses

     the ritual arson of hairdone

     the exiled snake of Saturday liquor

     the stranger danger of that funny smoke

     the untouched slick of just-roommates   Sure, just

     the stripped steeple of   sermons just

     the fevered climb of   organs yes

     the feral leap of   praise

A Financial Planner Asks about My Goals, or Golden Shovel with Cardi B's "Money"

Never touch-starved again, forever a chub-bellied baby sexed big
Skin a heatmapped catalog of hands still wet still grasping still blood-fat
Behind every steam-slammed door, playplush beds as good as checks
Whole home stitched with only these rooms, only this near-rip big
Kitchen table perfect island for the stranding, meals propped heaven-large
Backyard a honey-dripped grove named Eden, ripe land of no bills
Whatever drops first, spice-adorned, sauce slicked back-to-front
Splayed open slow, tempting a spill, grateful to be devoured like I'll
Make my giggling groommates, spit-tethered hips churned tender flip
Down smeared-open growls or whole wedding cakes or any drown we like
Just measure by the fistful how thick this slick can coat a sigh, add ten
And that'd be balm enough to dizzytrip my lonely and her cartwheels

Mr. Hotep Says #BlackLivesMatter and He'd Kill a Dyke

The dyke within
tires of
the nigger without

sick of rope
when the brick
calls her name.

Same blood
same alley

wrong hands
wrong headline

wrong barking pack
circling the same
hellmouth

same body
split, cracked
open.

Wrong balm
slicked
on the sin

wrong North
guiding the killer's
new heart

wrong village
tasked
with forgiveness

same torches
blackening
the door.

All the women
in this body
burn at once

no matter
how wrong
the fire

and oh god
the sound:
a chorus.

The notes
softer
in sum.

A dirge
for killer's
hands

as they
break
bread

for a lover
with half
this face

and twice
the room
for flame.

Love Letter from Pompeii

How many years since our ground

                  last split open and shook—remember

that quake made us dance

               without moving our feet? Our song

  is a crumbling world, all the bedrooms

                  unwalled and on fire—thank

  Vesuvius. They say it's why our temples keep

                     tipping. Say

the neck spills a death heat. Before the black,

                 red, red

                    everything.

  Would you call this *violence* or

                weather? I don't trust your hands, but I

believe your bite is guiltless as

              the rain. Would you call this *love*

or *the death heat*? If we must melt, can it be

                  from the inside out?

  Can they find our bones

          vined? My salt scorched into

                your teeth? Quick.

While we're still

     soft. Still thick grips and whole

               mouthfuls—I want to melt

  while it still feels good

        to scream.

• • • • •

The Lion Tamer's Daughter vs. the Whip

Bury me with you, master.
Coil me through you slit-to-slit,

toes splitting teeth, thighs a tongue,
head hip-deep, sweet godrest.

But master, those hands—
a gray soil bingeing seed,

a field of oil-black plums
writhing, worms for pits.

Give me purple bloat & burst,
sticky peel & maggot rain,

whole palm sprinting free just
to rot around my throat—

I'm made to be touched
this way.

One with the terror grip.
A once-dead thing

cracked alive.

no more white girls, or what i learned from Father

sure, your daddy hit you—once and not like mine:
all knuckle, leather, and the fear of God, divine right of kings
turned taxi drivers. your daddy hit like he'd been here generations,
never ran away from nothing just to be nobody. like he could be Jesus
'cause Jesus looks like him here. my Father hit like a nigerian's first wisconsin winter:

what kind of human survives through this? like on a good day, His name's a fresh spitwad
in some bank teller's scoff. you can hurt me like late for curfew, crashed the car.
i can hurt you like home's an ache no one believes. you inherited glut,
bloodsweet heart marbled prime, tender meat. i inherited hunger,
popped jaw all teeth, and Father taught me how to feast.

44 Questions to Ask While Bingeing

after Benji Hart

1. How many hands have touched this food?
2. What were their intentions?
3. How vast is the range?
4. What makes them hands at all?
5. How many seeds survived their births for this?
6. Did you count yourself?
7. From sprout to pluck, how many breaths old was the oldest?
8. What's become of its homeland?
9. How many breaths will it add to yours?
10. Or is this a thing that takes?
11. Which things were born dead for this?
12. Did you count yourself?
13. Which born free?
14. Which born food?
15. Is there a state in between?
16. How old was the well of that answer?
17. If governments and their signed scrolls are Plato's cave wall shadows, where is the real sun?
18. What's become of its homeland?
19. How many generations removed from the land are you?
20. What floor takes its place?
21. What is it built on top of?
22. Are the people who tended that place still alive?
23. Are there any living descendants?
24. Is their language still spoken on Earth?
25. If you heard it, would your feet twitch?
26. Or does dead mean gone?
27. How many gone things in your place?
28. Did you count yourself?
29. What does your body and the day it makes cost?
30. What is its price in gone things?
31. Is this sustainable? Better—regenerative?
32. Or will this make you the most gone thing alive?

33. Is God or the human the cave wall shadow?

34. Who says the shadow is nothing at all?

35. Are you still eating?

36. Who?

37. What for?

38. What have you grown in its place?

39. How much is enough?

40. Is enough a place or a count?

41. Is there a state in between?

42. Or does enough mean gone?

43. Did you enough yourself?

44. In the language of the oldest gone thing, how do you say devour?

catatonia mercy / or what i learned from mother

i was raised by the ghost who haunts the house i grew up in / she calls at least once a week / *are you okay?* / *yes it's sunny* / i say from the closet / curled between a suitcase and the wall / she's fourth generation spoiled fruit 'neath the poplars / born in the basement of a bombed-out church / i've inherited the snapped neck / the smoked lungs / the terror / *have you eaten?* / the ghost smooths her dress over a billowing cough / *yes* / i yell / fists stuffed into my mouth / i don't ask about Charleston / if she tastes the bullet meal / *are you lying?* / her voice is a whole choir burning / *i don't know* / my voice is the shot that missed the child / *we survive* / the ghost mistakes her chill for breath / *i know* / i lie / staring straight through my chest / and we / the lucky ones / have never known greater mercies

The Virus

Caught from PBS NewsHour

Note: This story   to include   the fatal

shot

stalled

When

social media   became

death   streamed live

Castile gasping for air

5 million times

who wandered away   living

with   injuries   people call

impossible,

mere   nuisance.

research   exposure to   black

trauma

combined with   a heightened sense of

America

study   viral

anguish,   the share

a sick sort of

witness.

enough,

just enough.

The News

eating   people

          the death Reign   certain

humanity   given to   gruesome

                                                            White people

          their children

conditioned to   call   a color

                                                            nightmare

          Avoiding Tamir

          in the park

grief brought   this   exhausting

                                                            sleep

protests   break

                                                            the rest of the world.

    I   disconnect.

                                                            nearly empty.

                                    a   symptom

● ● ● ● ●

Against Heaven

with "Goin' Up Yonder" and Louise Glück's Nobel Prize speech

I can take the pain whittling dad's body to the red balances *of his account*
The heartaches they bring: twin strokes, diabetes, ritual crucifixion *of his feelings and*
The comfort in knowing while he drives cab, there's engineers in Lagos with *his experience*
I'll soon be gone, college-flung debtchild taught empire *contains no blame*

As God gives me grace, I dump His dope, cut and flushed till I'm *no wish*
I'll run this race clean-sinning judge-hunting hex-lining a route *to revenge*
Until I see my savior in a city on fire, bank windows busted by Jesus *Himself*
Face to face with riot cops, tased to piss, tunic charged with *only the belief*

I'm goin' up yonder to jailbreak Cousin (everybody named *that in the perfect world*)
Goin' up yonder to repo mansions (Lil Black Boy swears *he has been promised*)
I'm goin' up yonder to the Michelin stars (cash my feast postdated *after death*)
Goin' up yonder to the Ivy plantation (hood dad so *he will be recognized*)

I'm goin' up yonder in a tux of knives, cursing in tongues—turn down *for what*
To be with my Lord? Tell the Wiz to guard his curtain—I know exactly what *He is*

Excerpt from *The Book of Oceans*

I.   Though the whyteman prefers his god alpha omega,
     I am neither the first nor the last:

II. I am the before and the after;

III. I am god enough to know them as the same.

IV. Though the whyteman prefers his god invisible
     and elsewhere, be still and know who I am:

V.   The great last flood of verse and fable;

VI. The horsemen's arrival on galloping waves;

VII. A seafloor worth of bones resurrected to churn
     this cauldron to a boil.

VIII. This is how it ends: one rising tide, an open mouth
      kissing you goodbye.

Theory of Plate Tectonics

for Regina

She says New England hoards college girls like cherries in its cheek,
tongue-tying legs to knots, making party tricks out of people.
Says it's an old currency, wads of tangled stems tumored
with unfinished bows. Says the quick ones learn to curl like ribbon.
The brave ones learn to run with their hands. The pretty ones knot
and knot into rope and callus, none of their blood stays long.
But half butane, half lemon juice, all pit, no skin, us sad ones
are a new fruit. I tell her we should shower more. Eat something
besides black pepper and rum. I tell her the teapot's melted
to the stove, the mugs chipped in hazardous places—dropped
from scalded hands to blades, stealing lips from our guests.
She reminds me we have no guests here. Just the half-dead boys
we've specialized in trapping, leggy never-giants too grateful to run.
Cups brimming with sliced smirks, kitchen table littered with scabs,
we pick over their charred parts: matchheads sawed from stems
with his sharpest key (ours now); a still-warm collarbone (ours now);
the lightbulb he almost smashed into her throat when he learned
not all flightless soft-bodied girls are fireflies (ours to shatter
in the rooftop shadows just like one of us). She tells me Paris
is glitter and ash this time of year, red-velvet gloved and scowled.
Tells me Cape Town paves its streets with wings that shimmy
for stray coins. Says she's got a naked man waiting in Havana
and his neighbor owes her seven cigarettes. She's been studying
plate tectonics. Whispering spells for Pangaea. Lighting candles
for the Great Rift Valley with bootleg magma from Kilimanjaro.
Branding Himalayas to her calves' Appalachia. Speed testing
smoke signals hitched to waves. She asks me the difference
between arson and wildfire. I say *arson* is chain-smoking
with her Tinder wax doll collection. *Wildfire* is misusing matches
as daylight. Should have said the difference depends on what's burning.
Such old bones for such new people, more cinder than marrow.
We feel safe in all the wrong places, most at home in flames.

prayer in child's pose

fuck your rose quartz! your incense-tune-forked vibes!
every god is a bloodsport crown
and light is no exception—
                              i'm sorry.
before this, i fell out of warrior pose
and cried for blunts, bacon, caramel cake,
deleting your number, quitting my job,
buying a gun with one bullet (do they sell less
than classroom packs? should i learn more
before the race war?) and i thought all this
as my grieving thighs
                        hit the floor.
        why not darkness?
some blessed ones rise and some of us sit,
witness. the priest hangs
from robes sewn by the village.
the poet, their twin, starves
naked and alone.
both fill books with all they know
of prayer.
                prayer!
tribe, stewards of my stuck-shut soul:
so long as we're Black, blue, and alive,
Big Holy twerks beneath a falling sky.
can't tell me darkness don't shine.

the oldest song

yusef says *this morning makes us the oldest song in any god's throat.* i dress this on a new love whose fingers dissolve time, who plumes me into a whole choir, reconstructs her jaw to fit the worship. but nightdreams call me a liar, show only your face. my blood tides to the timbre of your voice and nothing else. shut me up. bad news on the way, truth's fist halfway to my good eye, the bastard drunk in drawers stuttering *st-st-stay.* shut me up before i marry the fool again. shut me up before we aisle-run to you and your bride, dwayne wayne pleading *baby please.* i blame mercury for the retrograde. blame industry for snow heaped onto still-green leaves. blame lead in the pipes and plastic-piled oceans for this mile-deep thirst. shut me up before i tell you what my body found in that cavern, hell-singed, borrowed and begged. shut me up before the old no withers me down to the devil's chord again.

After We Ruin My Love's Heart, the God of Annihilation Prays Back to Me

O brick fist,

O scalpel-crowned

storm's eye, twitching

roach king, salivating

guardian of angels cast

into the blister-white void—

as devil-to-be, tell me: how has

that all-breath and sweet-mud heart earned

the ammonia cloud and rootshred of

you? whole home devoured.

your bed, blazing crash site, kept your

all-knuckle, unblooded

hands casket-still, ghost-

desire: malware mimicking

cool? praise

the body, now one burst seam.

ye treeless planet,

O frothing ocean of

my bleach and flame-

licked bone,

forged mirror:

what does one call a god

twinning the dark, your faith

with no worshippers? where's the

burnt silk

thread between freedom and death

my sweat-drenched slip,

when you're

the truest skin I know—

the last one left?

The Lonely Dream in Fevers

Did you hear the one about their teeth?

They were looking down a concrete road
toward a mountain toward the sky
when their teeth turned to pebbles in their head
then lead fillings coating the tongue
then ash then smoke then their whole body fire
then a single flame then the flicker gone
then just the road just the mountain just the sky.

Or that one about their cunt?

A green swamp steaming
the scaled and slimed life hissing croaking
a sweat choir gossiping between songs
vines for robes moss for robes river for robes
branches a thick webbed robe
and together they sang *hallelujah amen*
glory be this rain.

Their hair?

The December field
the cropless year
the cracked plow
the toolshed a splinter heap
the wind a house sweeper
the dishes flung to glittering blades
the apples wallpaper puree
the bark peeled the trees stripped
the sap pummeled out unleashed
pouring`pouring.

They wake cackling,
gums a bloody pulse.

They wake naked,
fist bloomed inside themself.

They wake bald,
throat packed with coconut oil.

They beg the night to bring a lover, all hands no face.
Night says *yes, child* and their skin thickens,
whole body callus, scalp to toe.

They beg the night to bring a balm.
Night says *yes, child* and their eyes are open
faucets, room the smallest sea.

They beg the night, let them drown,
let them drown drown drown.
Night says *yes, child.*

They wake.

• • • • •

The Lion Tamer's Daughter vs. Full Moon in Leo

Ha!

Can your whip make an ocean
sing its own lips to ribbons?

Are you maker of all the world's
mouths?

What you know about big game,
speck queen?

What you know about freedom,
ghost ghost? speck queen,

freedom be eight billion tongues
lapping whole cities up from root.

Freedom be a mouth open so wide,
its lips touch on the wrong side.

Everything's name,
song.

All the world's voice,
blue blue ribbon.

What your whip know about
blue blue?

What cage noise did your daddy
name you?

speck queen?
ghost ghost?

salt!

Soft & Beautiful Just for Me Relaxer, No-Lye Conditioning Creme, Children's Regular

DIRECTIONS

Snatch the could-be-girl-'cept-she-too-dark
-'cept-them-nigga-naps child by the braids.

Slice them open. Rake the comb through.
Cue the scalp pop, the scab-robed choir.

Teach the tribe dirge: staccato rip-rip
crescendo into sizzle and shred.

Litter the neck with butchered kinks,
a gutter-fur shawl, diseased offering.

Heat stroke, swamp drown, chemical spill,
decompose, exorcise, drag and prop

until brillo collapses, satin rises,
arabesques and curtsies with a snap.

Heaven's darkest halo is a high yellow.
On Earth at last, a crown is cast in black.

INGREDIENTS

Propylene Glycol (Antifreeze)
These winters nothing natural survives

Helianthus Annuus (Sunflower)
Half the wildlife extinct

Hydroxyethyl Cellulose (KY Jelly)
The rest tweaked to triple their bloom

Citronellol (Repellent)
Teach her to burn

Salvia Officinalis (Sage)
All smoke no fire

Aqua (Water)
Refuse to call God by name

WARNING

A child is made of water. A Black girl,
open flame. Product may catch fire.

Osun may wrestle from her kitchen,
snap your comb in two.

There may be no Black girls,
only burning gods.

There may be no Jesus,
just empire.

You may be both the army
and the scorched earth below.

DIRECTIONS

What was the Atlantic
before it became a graveyard?

Before crops meant auction blocks,
which dance brought the rain?

For best results:
cover her. Fall in praise.

Be cloudthick
and unpartable.

Be tangled,
skystuck waves.

At H&M, When Another Black Girl Asks If I Work Here

like my head wrap unfurled   flagged
a poached coast fashion   motherland magazine
colored girl cover girl   bent over   nameless
coupons and full spread inside

a poached coast fashion   motherland magazine
mannequin dunked in chocolate   pretzel posed
couponed full and spread inside
deboned   battered   chicken-lard fried

mannequin dunked in chocolate   pretzel posed
by my work-thick hands   knuckle cracked
deboned   battered   chicken-lard fried
minimum-wage manicure lickety-spit shined

by my work-thick hands   knuckle-cracked
plastic hanger cotton picked   sweat dazzling
minimum-wage manicure lickety-spit shined
can I help you can I help you can I help

plastic hanger cotton picked? sweat dazzling?
snatching exactly *that* off the rack?
can I help you can I help you can I help
house nigga hips popping hard left-right?

snatching exactly *that* off the rack
wallets fat with daddy's teeth
house nigga hips popping hard-right left
to mama's gospel Muzaked godless

wallets fat with daddy's teeth
cavitied currency without a country
to ammo godless   spells go Muzak
hourly bruised and blue-collared blackest

cavitied currency without a country
like my head wrap unfurled   flagged
hourly bruised blue and collared blackest
colored girl cover bot   never girl   nameless

Undelivered Message to the Sky: November 9, 2016

You were in my dream last night. Titanic falling.
Every cop siren pocking your blue. Shots fired
straight above my head by trembling men, then

a hot lead rain.   You still sank,
and all the creatures bowed—except the humans.
We broke the land screaming then shattered the sound.

When I woke up, I felt it. A twitching in my teeth.
The rumble of a nearby rapture.   I opened the blinds
and a pack of white women were wailing down 45th,

crying into potholes, writhing in the street
like worms. One saw me.   Wails pitched
to a weapons-grade *sorry sorry sorry*

so sorry we're sorry and I wished Yemoja
would sling an ocean out my throat.
But all I had was English—

blindfolds, trick knives. No real magic.
Nothing in their language makes them
disappear.   That's why

the guns and cages. Why
they cut our tongues.

Because we would call,
and you would come.

Depression Proposes to Me Again

She was born for the fifth time in 1990
from pork fat and church-boy jazz.

Says she was built by sun-blacked backs
in a city lost inside its own mouth.

The Midwest taught her all about heartbreak:
the speed paint color fades,

how beauty abandoned is beauty begrudged,
refuses to pose again.

Swallowed a house before the fourth time.
Wanted a birthplace no one could take.

Whole joint's the color of my mother's blood.
Runoff seafoam inside. Oil-dumped coral outside.

Asks if I like best the quiet of a field or a forest.
Asks if I would paint the walls jade or evergreen.

Says we're not island drift but Wedded Seed.
Says I am God Root and she is Good Soil

like she was born for the last time.
Like she found a whole city in my mouth.

Against Heaven

In Chicago, a Steep Rise in Suicide Among Black People

Halfway   to   Graves,

North Lawndale   kids line up to buy

calls   to   death's   residents.

a boy,   9 years old

pays   a buffet of   scraps

for   a

helpline   to

the   city of waiting rooms

surveys the

suicide

district.

The   Black   deal or

a small

lead   dress.

the

sidetracked

crease   With   conversation,

speak

B ack

something out there trying to get us

life   a

red   ear

in   the   call
cord,

time   back

to
work

in

s   l   ow   motion

blunt

wave   coming to

a Steep Rise

• • • • •

The Lion Tamer's Daughter vs. the Ledge

O taxi glass, O broken fall, be soprano, be alto.
Give me sea sharp, give me doh doh doh, give mi fa *so*?
O gravity, slip soft. Lie with this sorry child
       before they soulsplint & ugly up this here garden.
O slurred night, be witness, be whole sky peopled,
       sagging, buttons gaped & threatening *pop*!
O blanket tent stonebones, be a ledger.
(How much blood does this sorry child owe?
Make it twenty-eight cavitied teeth,
       twelve still attached to gum?
Half a spine & nineteen fistfuls of *salt*?)
Tailored crew cut 3L be a *so*?
Euro backpack gap year, be a Snapchat ohmygoding
Popcorn-passing crowd, with your one long pointed finger,
       be strangers still.
Shivers & splints, O gaping, breathless skies,
       be siblings now.
O weave, dread & head wrap, be a praise twerk smudging.
O coven, keep this child's eyes in a jar.
Stuff pillows with their kinks.
Make soaps from their cheeks.
O coven, fry their brains in butter & sage, grease your scalps,
       then eat.
Your fingernails will spike long as sugarcane.
Your skin will glow garnet & gold.
Dig a garden, each eyelash: seed.
Watch the medicine grow.

you must believe in spring

even the black ground's aching and ashy, colonized by a pasty snow—
thief socking you to sleep before blaming the dark.

virus news sweeps your screens and your blue-lit mind
fixes on the frozen lake, closest lover to curl inside.

you would trade a skull of yes/no for quiet, two slushed thoughts
per foot below, but there it goes dewing the frost of your plan:

star witness to original sin, atlantic turned accomplice,
tongues flung overboard for charming its rise, there it goes:

that same sun cupping your cheek begs *thaw*—
and a seed survives their winter. a lost spell buds.

Eulogy for the Voice in My Head

He died as he lived: tongue in my mouth, whipping me from the inside out.
Kill yourself, then we were in the kitchen rinsing the knives. *Kill yourself,*
then on our knees picking wet pills off tile. Then strangers clawed us
from the train track, but a slippery sleeve. Then out for three days,

on a plane on a panel explaining the political good of Black joy,
digging his fingernails into our thigh for mispronouncing *hierarchal,*
for not connecting Jesus-dot to Master-dot, for my unslit throat,

sham offering. He died as he lived. As real as imagined.
Raw flesh hammered to plain wood posts. Spoiling in the sun
while I sucked the splinters from my palm, sure I killed a child of God
as the others dropped their plagues and played, forgiving me.

The Lonely Sleep through Winter

I say *hunger* and mean your hands bitten to boneseed,
bandaged with bedsheet and the night while two states over
a mouth—ready soil—says your name. Next June's lover
speaks the harvest: your rich, vowel-tender song

but for the neighbor. More *hello* than *amen*. Not yet
a whole book of psalms. Choose this. Not your bare room.
Your self-vacancies. Unlearn empire's blackness:
night spun savage, space cast empty when really

a balm slicks the split between stars. Really
hipthick spirits moonwalk across the lake ice.
Maps to every heaven gauze the trees in velvet
between that greenbright spectacle of bud and juice

and dust—I'm saying there's no such thing
as nothing. Try and try, you'll never disappear.
I say *hunger*, mean hands you think empty
though everywhere, even the dark, heaves.

Dendrochronology of This Want

Count the pimpled genitalia of sex-ed fame
       multiplied by every high school in Wisconsin

Add the ninth graders cast as pus-to-be
       instead of storm's eye: empty bellied, ravenous

Count the days my mother wondered where her clitoris was
       multiplied by the year she stopped asking

Add the Sundays pastor named Eve blight
       multiplied by the aunties' amens

And the deacon eyes needled through my stockings
And the weeks a body starves down to one closed fist
       multiplied by the dances too Black for corsage
       just Black enough for 808 bonegrind
       white-boy palm lines burned into hips
       ring-aged like tree crown sawed from trunk

Count every gender I refused for this branding

Measure the spectrum of unkissed

Calculate the surface area of skin
turned dust, my coat for twenty winters

       Holes in every pocket. I'd learned to beg—

       How many crumbs on the road to you?

           Measure the sine wave of this gasp
           Distance between trough and peak

Angle between eye centered and rolled
The shiver's velocity

Each second the body was lost
magnified to the tenth power

of the body returned
and returned
and returned

Against Heaven

double golden shovel with Sade and Belinda Carlisle

If gigglesoaked, Henny-leaned, Young M.A's *OOOUUU* sweat down to its nekkid *ooh*,
you ripen apart till tenderqueer innards drip and dangle from fuckboi halves then baby,
were you to waft my way, bright peach begging to cobbler, let heat do what it do—
mine gut-pent and wasted, sun born to sweet the orchard of you.

If forgiveness, uncoupled from the cross at our jugular, was a song we could know,
you and I against innocence in a red karaoke duet of fessed mess then what
were slights to scar the verses, cheats to bloody the bridge? The chorus, that's
mine: *There is a balm in Gilead.* Sticky resin turned perfume, and we've mucked a grove's worth.

I clown for you. Two-step to trap shea-buttered, lavender-spliffed with you and *ooh*
wouldn't we get swept out this Apollo, ancestors booing our bit's thin heaven?
Want a blue blaze snuffed in every realm. To misabolish and refuse your rule is
to pawn my only heirloom, blood for Sandman's broom. I toggle fool-to-fool for a

go at mercy, December fists blooming to rainbow strobes, dancefloor a place
to practice mesh and lace and rope and strap, our binding, our betting on
heaven as our circling set to crash, ripping pavement up to rewild Earth.

Polyamory Defense #324

Master of No Chill dates the Superintendent of Chest Pain County
who's married to a forest turned endless blaze
who's fucking a planet eighty percent gilded ash—
that part's a mess, but the body's more riddle
than liar. The body is just information.
Breath nowhere breath vanished means
I miss you, please touch me. Sometimes more
I miss touch, sometimes more *you please me.*
More *please me.* More *you* and *you* and *you*
are more than bomb shelters, let's baba a village,
warm our bodies back to real hearthed homes.
But where's the love poem for me, my partner,
their partner, our lovers and their rented doms?
No hymns, no church. Shoulders our altars.
Like everything we need, impossible.
Then imagined. Then desired.
Then made by trembling hands.
Gods bless the houses this love builds.

Goodbye Letter to My Lover's Wife

To the one who begged for no more guests and carved a kitchen chair for me anyway:

I took a seat at your overturned table, legs snapped and trembling.
Licked his fingers while you stomped the dishes back to sand.
Cried in closets for three days before you asked where I'd gone.

He held me like he was carrying bills from the mailbox to the trash,
but I ~~love him like it'd make my mother~~ sing ~~again,~~
~~turn~~ my ~~father's voice to nothing but~~ apologies.

You I could watch fall in a well and for a moment, stand still. Dream.
But the neighbors know your shout. Make curfews of it like streetlights.
Our man tunes his heart to this pitch then thinks he serenades me—

~~I know that one. My mother's last song.~~
They'll say I ran out shoeless, sand still in my hair.

Some people can't love with the knives put away.
Now I know there are worse lives than the lonely.

I open my hands: praise, a planet.

Everywhere I lie, my wedding bed.

A Wedding, or What We Unlearned from Descartes

Beloved, last night I doused us in good bourbon,
struck a match between our teeth, slid the lit head
lip to chest, throat zippered open and spilling.
Our union demands a sacrifice. Take my masks—
my wretched, immaculate children. Sharp smiles
bored with cavities. Braids thick with hair
slashed off lovers as they slept. The masks grew limbs
and danced, so last night, to the fire—plank pushed,
cackling as they bubbled and split. Then dreamless dark.
Then mercy, somehow, morning reached for me.
Sun found us swaddled in sweat-through sheets—
gauze and salve while night wore off. O body,
always healing despite me. O body, twin spy
tasked against my plot to rush the dying,
guardian of the next world's sweets, yes,
I'll lick this salt. Yes, I'll wait our turn
because today we hold hands, mother
each other, bathe in warm coconut oil.
Our union, our long baptism. O body,
all I forced you to know of thirst. Yes
body, you are owed a whole lake. Yes
body, I'll kiss our wrists, hold them
to our ears and spend our days
losing to the waves.

free fucked

verb, never passive

: to meditate before you read the news

: to lose six rainy days smiling at the neighbors, picking wet pennies off the ground

: to skip the news

: to write a poem about their shoulders, then fall asleep, two fingers inside yourself

: to read the news

: to pray to your neighbors

: to know you have never been a brain in a jar

: to learn we are bodies welding crowns for other bodies

: to feel crowns are made by hands

: to taste hands are water and sugar and know they should return

: to make good practice of this melt

: to spill from the bath

: to unhinge your front door

: to feed your body to the falling sky

planet fka the lion tamer's daughter, mapped

my father's open palm, drum taut, all war song.

                                                    crown of lye, barrette & braid.

two chords plucked out my mother's throat,
wrapped in foil, hurled off a lake bluff.

                                                    sink full of the boys' dishes
                                                    & my wet, shriveled hands.

                      all this, sea:
                                bruise-blue, ghost-thick.

          & there:

                                            somewhere between chicago & home,
                              my third skin scorched onto a highway,

                        pipe tucked in my boot,
                gina's breath singed to my neck.

the sin of her,

                        my first good meal.

                                    the entire tongue.
                                        every finger & lash, sweet lightning.

                  root-to-crown gospel.
              cheeks, full cauldrons.
              whole heart, witch witch witch.

                                                  & there,

land:

      a bed I built myself,
      fresh country.

there,
  sky:

    endless choir
      of cocoa

   & rose &
      my name.

Against Heaven

I used to pray to a man-faced god.
Kept his whip beneath my bed.

Set alarms for daybreak lashings.
Pressed white cotton to the flay.

Made flags of the bloodsoak.
Raised them from my window.

Called this *worship.*

Dreamt heaven a jury small as a county
where nobody looked like me.

Winged bailiffs plucked my cuffs
to trap my cousin in a hot coal cage.

Called this roulette *freedom,*
licking my raw wrists.

Which kill blew my tatters down.
Peeled me to the blackest jade.

Remothered me to the squad car blaze.
Loot and shard my siblings now.

Which kill. Forgive me.
I feared the devil's prison.

Misfaithed the sheriff
in the sky. Why.

Which kill. Forgive me
family, I miscountried—

our swarming, anthem
of my true homeland.

Heaven and hell
are the same empire

half-slipped, gasping,
clutching our hems.

Ungoverned by the lie,
with fists and flames,

we cleave.

NOTES

In "How to Fornicate," the phrase "Blessed Queers" carries the spirit of Mark Aguhar's poem "Litanies to My Heavenly Brown Body."

The golden shovel form emerged from the mind of Terrance Hayes as an homage to Gwendolyn Brooks. His poem "The Golden Shovel" ends each line with a word from Brooks's "We Real Cool." Though *Against Heaven*'s golden shovels do not draw their language from Brooks's poetry, they are indebted to her work and legacy, particularly the poem "To the Young Who Want to Die": "Graves grow no green that you can use. / Remember, green's your color. You are Spring."

"Sunday Closet" was inspired by a line in Dionne Brand's "Ossuary I" ("the casual homicides of dresses").

"The Virus" is a blackout of "When black death goes viral, it can trigger PTSD-like trauma," a *PBS NewsHour* article by Kenya Downs published July 22, 2016.

"the oldest song" borrows a line from Yusef Komunyakaa's "Providence."

"Against Heaven (Halfway to Graves)" is a blackout of "In Chicago, a Steep Rise in Suicide Among Black People," an article in the *Trace* by Lakeidra Chavis published July 25, 2020.

"you must believe in spring" is titled after the song as performed by Bill Evans.

"Dendrochronology of This Want" was written in response to an "In Surreal Life" writing workshop prompt by Shira Erlichman.

ACKNOWLEDGMENTS

Thank you to the editors of the following publications for homing early versions of these poems:

"Voice Clear As," The Academy of American Poets' *Poem-a-Day*; "44 Questions to Ask While Bingeing" and "Love Poem -1: Chicago (CST) to Bangalore (GMT+5:30)," *American Poets Magazine*; "Mr. Hotep Says #BlackLivesMatter and He'd Kill a Dyke" and "catatonia mercy / or what i learned from mother," *Apogee Journal*; "Against Heaven (There's Earth)," *The Atlantic*; "Against Heaven (I can take the pain)," *Beloit Poetry Journal*; "After We Ruin My Love's Heart, the God of Annihilation Prays Back to Me," "Against Heaven (If gigglesoaked)," *Black Warrior Review*; "Soft & Beautiful Just for Me Relaxer, No-Lye Conditioning Creme, Children's Regular," *BOAAT*; "Undelivered Message to the Sky: November 9, 2016," *Boston Review*; "Eulogy for the Voice in My Head," *Dgёku*; "A Wedding, or What We Unlearned from Descartes," *Guernica*; "you must believe in spring," *Jewish Currents*; "no more white girls, or what i learned from Father" and "At H&M, When Another Black Girl Asks If I Work Here," *Kweli Journal*; "The Lion Tamer's Daughter vs. the Ledge," *The Massachusetts Review*; "The Lonely Dream in Fevers," *Nat. Brut*; "How to Fornicate," *The Nation*; "Voice Clear As," *Poem-a-Day*; "A Financial Planner Asks about My Goals, or Golden Shovel with Cardi B's 'Money,'" *Poetry*; "black as:" *Redivider*; "Dendrochronology of This Want" and "Theory of Plate Tectonics," *The Rumpus*; "the oldest song," *them.*; "The Lonely Sleep through Winter," *TriQuarterly*; "Polyamory Defense #324" and "prayer in child's pose," *Underblong*; "Love Letter from Pompeii," *Waxwing*; "planet fka the lion tamer's daughter, mapped" and "free fucked," *Winter Tangerine*.

"Soft & Beautiful Just for Me Relaxer, No-Lye Conditioning Creme, Children's Regular" also appears in *Best New Poets 2019* (University of Virigina Press, 2019) and *The Echoing Ida Collection* (Feminist Press, 2021). "At H&M, When Another Black Girl Asks if I Work Here" and "Mr. Hotep Says #BlackLivesMatter and He'd Kill a Dyke" also appear in *The BreakBeat Poets Vol. 2: Black Girl Magic* (Haymarket Books, 2018). "A Wedding, or What We Unlearned from Descartes" also appears in *A Garden of Black Joy: Global Poetry from the Edges of Liberation and Living* (Wise Ink, 2020). "planet fka the lion tamer's daughter, mapped" also appears, with a different title, in *Sweeter Voices Still: An LGBTQ Anthology from Middle America* (Belt Publishing, 2021).

Claudia Rankine and the Academy of American Poets, thank you for your path-clearing *yes*. Graywolf Press, especially Chantz Erolin and Kiki Nicole, thank you for bringing the best version of this book out of me and into the world. Llanor Alleyne, thank you for sharing your gorgeous *Seraphina* for this cover.

Thank you to the teachers whose brief but powerful lessons shaped this work. Special shout-out to Samiya Bashir, Angelina Cicero, and Ronaldo V. Wilson.

Thank you to the cultural workers who ground my practice in truth telling, liberation, and radical imagination. Special shout-out to the writers and artists of Echoing Ida and the Trans Day of Resilience project.

Thank you to the stewards of my first poetry homes, Boston University's Speak for Yourself and the Boston Poetry Slam. Thank you to the communities of practice that held me between now and then, especially Kearney Street's Interdisciplinary Writer's Lab 2016, my Winter Tangerine workshop crews, Team Bashir of Tin House Summer Workshop 2019, and the feral babes of Pink Door 2019.

Thank you to the homies and beloveds. Shout-out to Benji, Bianca, Derrick, Diana, Dinah, Hakeem, Hannah, Janna, Jasmine, Micah, Mika, Rosa, Shaka, and Taofiki. Sanam, thank you for being this book's first and most trusted reader. Ella, thank you for talking me off the ledge. Mom, I know I ran wild, but thanks for always letting me come back to you.

A kiss to the ever-expanding universe of magical Black queerdos. Heaven is wherever we are.

Peace to the lovers and believers. Power to the next-world builders. All my gratitude to our wild faiths.

Reader, thank you for spending some of your precious time on Earth with this work.

KEMI ALABI is the author of *Against Heaven,* winner of the Academy of American Poets First Book Award, and coeditor of *The Echoing Ida Collection.* Their work has been published in *Poetry,* the *Nation, The BreakBeat Poets Vol. 2, Best New Poets 2019,* and elsewhere. The recipient of the 2020 Beacon Street Prize, Alabi has received support from MacDowell, Tin House, and Pink Door. Born on a Sunday in July, they live in Chicago, Illinois.

The text of *Against Heaven* is set in Arno Pro.
Book design by Rachel Holscher.
Composition by Bookmobile Design and Digital
Publisher Services, Minneapolis, Minnesota.
Manufactured by McNaughton & Gunn on acid-free,
100 percent postconsumer wastepaper.